WALLKILL PUBLIC LIBRARY

3 2843 00012 1413

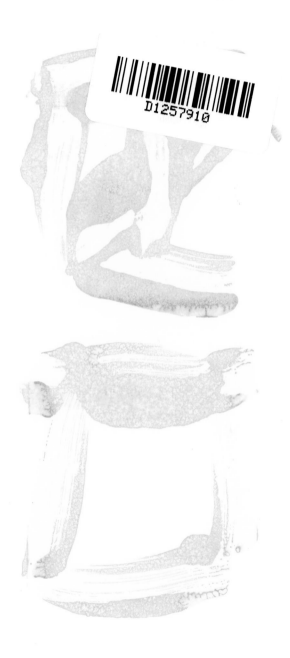

Visual Geography Series®

EGYPT
...in Pictures

Prepared by
Stephen C. Feinstein

Lerner Publications Company
Minneapolis

Copyright © 1988 by Lerner Publications Company. Revised and updated 1989, 1992.

All rights reserved. International copyright secured. No part of this book may be reproduced, stored in a retrieval system, or transmitted in any form or by any means—electronic, mechanical, photocopying, recording, or otherwise—without the prior written permission of the publisher, except for the inclusion of brief quotations in an acknowledged review.

Courtesy of American Lutheran Church

The domesticated camel is still widely used in Egypt.

This book is an all-new edition in the Visual Geography Series. Previous editions were published by Sterling Publishing Company, New York City. The text, set in 10/12 Century Textbook, is fully revised and updated, and new photographs, maps, charts, and captions have been added.

LIBRARY OF CONGRESS CATALOGING-IN-PUBLICATION DATA

Feinstein, Steve.
   Egypt in pictures / prepared by Steve Feinstein.
   p. cm. — (Visual geography series)
   Rev. ed. of: Egypt in pictures / by Camille Mirepoix.
   Includes index.
   Summary: Introduces the history, geography, economy, government, culture, and people of the Arab nation whose history dates back more than 5000 years.
   ISBN 0-8225-1840-6 (lib. bdg.)
   1. Egypt. [1. Egypt.] I. Mirepoix, Camille, Egypt in pictures. II. Title. III. Series: Visual geography series (Minneapolis, Minn.)
DT46.F44 1988   87-27038
962'.05—dc19   CIP
                                                  AC

International Standard Book Number: 0-8225-1840-6
Library of Congress Catalog Card Number: 87-27038

VISUAL GEOGRAPHY SERIES®

Publisher
Harry Jonas Lerner
Associate Publisher
Nancy M. Campbell
Senior Editor
Mary M. Rodgers
Editor
Gretchen Bratvold
Assistant Editors
Dan Filbin
Kathleen S. Heidel
Illustrations Editor
Karen A. Sirvaitis
Consultants/Contributors
Stephen C. Feinstein
Sandra K. Davis
Designer
Jim Simondet
Cartographer
Carol F. Barrett
Indexer
Sylvia Timian
Production Manager
Gary J. Hansen

Independent Picture Service

Murals adorn the walls of ancient Egyptian tombs.

Acknowledgments

Title page photo by Drs. A. A. M. van der Heyden, Naarden, the Netherlands.

Elevation contours adapted from *The Times Atlas of the World*, seventh comprehensive edition (New York: Times Books, 1985).

3 4 5 6 7 8 9 10 97 96 95 94 93 92

Courtesy of American Lutheran Church

More than 21 million Egyptians—40 percent of the population—are under the age of 15.

Contents

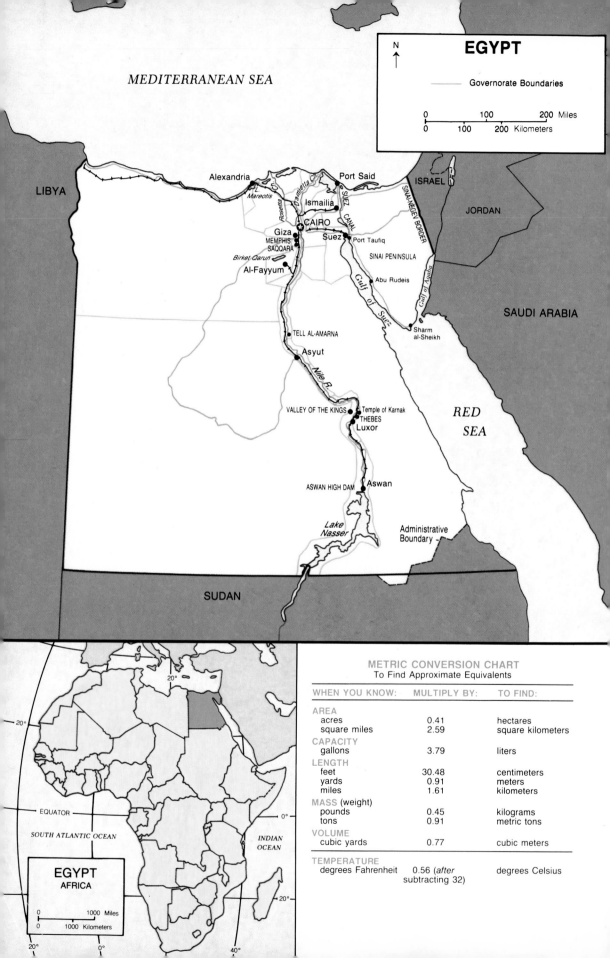

MEDITERRANEAN SEA

EGYPT

Governorate Boundaries

0   100   200 Miles
0   100   200 Kilometers

LIBYA

Alexandria
Port Said
ISRAEL
Mareotis
Damietta Ch.
Rosetta
Ismailia
JORDAN
CAIRO
SUEZ
CANAL
SINAI–NEGEV BORDER
Giza
Suez
MEMPHIS
Port Taufiq
SAQQARA
Birket Qarun
SINAI PENINSULA
Al-Fayyum
Abu Rudeis
Gulf of Aqaba
SAUDI ARABIA
Gulf of Suez

TELL AL-AMARNA
Asyut

Sharm
al-Sheikh

Nile R.

RED
SEA

VALLEY OF THE KINGS
Temple of Karnak
THEBES
Luxor

ASWAN HIGH DAM
Aswan

Lake
Nasser

Administrative
Boundary

SUDAN

EGYPT
AFRICA

20°
20°
EQUATOR
0°
SOUTH ATLANTIC OCEAN
INDIAN
OCEAN
20°
20°
0°
40°

0   1000 Miles
0   1000 Kilometers

METRIC CONVERSION CHART
To Find Approximate Equivalents

WHEN YOU KNOW:	MULTIPLY BY:	TO FIND:
AREA		
acres	0.41	hectares
square miles	2.59	square kilometers
CAPACITY		
gallons	3.79	liters
LENGTH		
feet	30.48	centimeters
yards	0.91	meters
miles	1.61	kilometers
MASS (weight)		
pounds	0.45	kilograms
tons	0.91	metric tons
VOLUME		
cubic yards	0.77	cubic meters
TEMPERATURE		
degrees Fahrenheit	0.56 (*after* subtracting 32)	degrees Celsius

Only a small portion of Egypt's land-mass is suitable for farming. As a result, almost all of the country's rapidly expanding population lives along the banks of the Nile River, making throngs of people a common sight in urban areas.

Courtesy of Kay Chernush/Agency for International Development

Introduction

With 5,000 years of recorded history, Egypt evokes many images. Only archaeological remnants, many with still-unexplained uses, remain from ancient Egypt. Since this early period of rule by the Pharaohs (kings), foreign influences have dominated Egypt's history. In 30 B.C., Egypt became part of the Roman Empire, a period of rule that would last for another 600 years, until Arabs entered the region. For the past 1,400 years, Egypt has been one of the great centers of Arab culture, politics, and religion.

Present-day Egypt faces many challenges. Cairo, the largest city in Africa, contained a population of about 15 million people in the early 1990s. The overcrowding of this city, as well as the overall rise

5

In November 1977, Egyptian president Anwar el-Sadat *(left)* spoke before Israel's Knesset (parliament) in an effort to begin peaceful relations between Arabs and Jews.

Courtesy of Israel Government Press Office

in the country's population, contributes to the problems modern Egypt must confront.

Overpopulation is not Egypt's only challenge. It has had a history of warfare with Israel, a nation formed in 1948 to create a homeland for the Jewish people. In 1979, however, Egypt became the first Arab state to make peace with Israel. Tensions thus increased between Egypt and its Arab neighbors—as well as among its own people. These tensions escalated in 1990 and 1991, when Egypt supported the United States, many European nations, and some other Arab states in opposing Iraq's invasion of Kuwait. Egypt sent about 30,000 troops to Saudi Arabia as part of an Arab fighting force.

As a result of Egypt's participation in the anti-Iraq coalition, foreign aid increased, and lenders erased some foreign debts. These moves have boosted Egypt's economy, which was struggling to make ends meet. Most Egyptians hope that their country will have a strong role in shaping events in the Arab world without endangering economic progress.

Courtesy of Agency for International Development

The Suez Canal, which connects the Red Sea with the Mediterranean Sea, has been an object of national and international concern since its construction in the mid-nineteenth century. In fact, control of trade routes in the canal zone has affected political affairs in Europe and the Middle East.

Photo by Drs. A. A. M. van der Heyden, Naarden, the Netherlands

Although level desert characterizes much of Egypt's terrain, rugged mountains rise along the Red Sea and in the Sinai Peninsula, and bluffs of limestone, sandstone, and granite flank the Nile.

1) The Land

Egypt lies in the northeastern corner of Africa at the point where the African and Asian continents meet. The Mediterranean and Red seas form natural water boundaries on the north and east, respectively, and straight lines make up the western frontier with Libya and the southern boundary with Sudan. These boundaries are not accidental. Although Egypt has a long history, its present size was determined mainly by the British during the colonial period from the 1880s until the 1920s.

Egypt has an area of 386,900 square miles—about equal in size to the states of Texas and California combined. Although the country is large, only about 4 percent of its land is suitable for farming—a fact that has dominated life in Egypt for centuries. The fertile territory lies along the Nile River, stretching north from Aswan and including the Nile Delta. Ninety-five percent of the population lives near the banks of the Nile. The rest of the country is desert, which new technology is slowly changing into productive farmland. The country can be divided into four main regions—the valley and delta of the Nile, the Western Desert, the Eastern Desert, and the Sinai Peninsula.

Photo by Andrew E. Beswick

Two boys fish in the calm waters of the Nile River near the town of Luxor.

The Nile River and Delta

Beginning in Tanzania, the Nile River flows northward through Uganda, Sudan, and Egypt and empties into the Mediterranean. In Egypt, the Nile Valley is a green strip that is 10 miles across at its widest point before it reaches Cairo, where it widens into the fields and sandbars of the delta. In this triangular region at the mouth of the Nile, the waterway splits into several channels. Its two main channels are the Damietta and Rosetta, named for the cities at their mouths. Silt deposited by these and other tributaries makes the delta the most fertile region of the country. It is 100 miles long and, at the Mediterranean coast, 155 miles wide. Four shallow, salty lakes extend along the delta's Mediterranean border.

Almost all of Egypt's farmland lies along its 960-mile stretch of the Nile.

South from Cairo, the Nile Valley is lined with cliffs of granite, sandstone, and limestone. For centuries this portion of the valley has been referred to as Upper Egypt, and the delta has been known as Lower Egypt. The southernmost section of the Nile Valley is part of a region called Nubia, which extends from Sudan north to the city of Aswan.

Deserts

The Western, or Libyan, Desert is part of the great Sahara, which covers about two-thirds of Egypt and averages 600 feet above sea level. Some highlands, however, such as the Jilf al-Kabir Plateau, rise to 3,000 feet. The Western Desert has vast hollows, including the Qattara Depression, which at 440 feet below sea level is the lowest point in Africa. A lake, Birket

Qarun, fills another depression north of the town of Al-Fayyum. A huge, sandy area within the Western Desert is referred to as the Great Sand Sea.

The Eastern Desert, often called the Arabian Desert, is also part of the Sahara and extends east from the Nile. Separated from the Nile Valley by sharp cliffs, the Eastern Desert rises gradually to a range of jagged, volcanic mountains with peaks over 7,000 feet high along the Red Sea.

Dry riverbeds, called wadis, cut deep channels across the Eastern Desert, giving it a very irregular surface. Occasionally during winter rains, water flows through these wadis. The southern edge of this region is known as the Nubian Desert, which extends into Sudan.

The Sinai Peninsula is separated from the rest of Egypt by the Gulf of Suez—which is an arm of the Red Sea—and by the Suez Canal. The peninsula is flanked

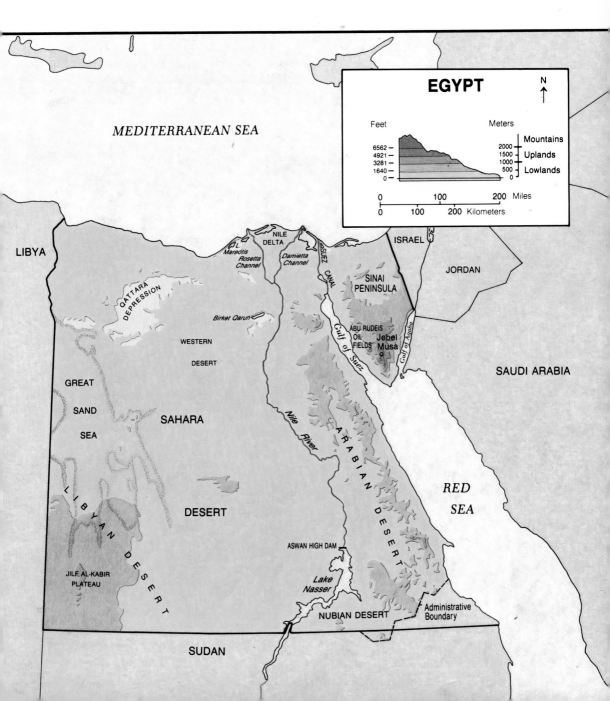

by the Gulf of Aqaba, which is another extension of the Red Sea, and by Israel on the east. Geographically, the Sinai Peninsula is part of southwestern Asia rather than of Africa.

A flat, sandy desert in the north, the peninsula consists of mountainous desert in the south and contains Egypt's highest peak, Jebel Katherina (8,652 feet). Nearby, rising 7,497 feet above sea level, stands Jebel Musa (Arabic for "Mountain of Moses"), which is considered by some to be the Mount Sinai on which, according to the Bible's Old Testament, Moses received the Ten Commandments.

The Aswan High Dam

In 1970 the Aswan High Dam was completed to control flooding of the Nile River. The backed-up waters of the Nile formed Lake Nasser, which stretches 150 miles south and reaches into Sudan. Water stored in the artificial lake has irrigated an additional one million acres of land for cultivation. Some people claim that the dam saved Egypt from the famine that ravaged eastern Africa, especially Ethiopia, during 1985 and 1986. An additional benefit from the dam is the vast quantity of electricity generated by its hydroelectric plant.

Despite these improvements, however, some Egyptians point out problems with the Aswan High Dam. For example, ecologists are concerned about the changes in climate and regional ecology caused by Lake Nasser. The lake has a high evaporation rate, which adds moisture to the air and could change the climate in southern

Courtesy of Steve Feinstein

Formed after the construction of the Aswan High Dam, Lake Nasser has flooded a number of famous archaeological sites, including Abu Simbel, the location of two rock temples built for Ramses II in the thirteenth century B.C. The structures have since been moved to higher ground.

Independent Picture Service

The arid expanse of the Western Desert is almost uninhabited. Only a few oases (fertile areas) exist, where shallow wells tap the underground water supply.

Egypt. Others suggest that slowing the flow of the Nile deprives farmers of the precious mud that came with the annual flood and destroys the shrimp population in the eastern Mediterranean. Furthermore, Egyptian industrial growth may soon require more electricity than the dam can provide.

Climate

Egypt has a dry climate throughout the year, with a hot season from May to September and a cool season from November to March. The country depends almost entirely on water from the Nile River and from wells. Even the Mediterranean coast, where the most rain falls, averages only

Independent Picture Service

Some nomadic Bedouin peoples *(above)* still travel Egypt's Eastern Desert, locating fresh water and grazing land for the animals they raise. Nubian villagers *(right)* resettled along the banks of Lake Nasser when construction of the Aswan High Dam caused flooding in their villages.

Independent Picture Service

11

eight inches of precipitation a year. Cairo receives only about one inch of rain per year, and many Egyptians who live in the southern part of the country have never seen rain.

During the summer the temperature in the desert at noon may exceed 110° F, but it drops sharply after sunset, so that evenings are cool. Cooling winds that blow from the Mediterranean moderate average summer temperatures near the coast. In this area temperatures range between 80°

Courtesy of Steve Feinstein
A single date palm tree may yield as much as 600 pounds of fruit in one year.

and 90° F. The winters are mild with clear sunny days and cool nights. Winter temperatures range from 55° to 70° F. Desert temperatures, however, can be much colder during the winter.

Hot, dry desert winds called khamsins occasionally blow in from the Sahara, bringing with them an extreme rise in temperature and low humidity. These storms carry dust and sand and can damage crops.

Flora and Fauna

Because of Egypt's dry climate, vegetation is confined largely to the Nile Valley, the delta, and desert oases (fertile areas). The most common native tree is the date palm. Others include the sycamore, acacia, and

Independent Picture Service
The multicolored butterfly finch is native to East African countries and can be seen in parts of Egypt. One of many species of primarily seed-eating birds, butterfly finches are likely to be seen in large flocks.

12

Delicate marine vegetation grows in the Red Sea, off the eastern coast of Egypt.

Photo by Drs. A. A. M. van der Heyden, Naarden, the Netherlands

Independent Picture Service

Inhabiting the plains and deserts of Africa, the wolflike jackal feeds mostly on what remains of the kill that other animals have left behind. By cleaning up these carcasses, the jackal helps to prevent the outbreak of disease within the animal community.

carob. Eucalyptus and various fruit-bearing trees have been introduced from foreign countries. In the rich soil of the delta, grapes, vegetables, and flowers—such as lotuses, jasmines, and roses—thrive. In the desert, alfa grass and several kinds of thorn plants can be found. Although papyrus once grew all along the Nile and was harvested for making paper, it now grows only in southernmost Egypt.

Snakes that are native to Egypt include the poisonous Egyptian cobra and the horned viper. Lizards are numerous. Although the hippopotamus and crocodile were common in both Upper and Lower Egypt during ancient times, they are now found only in Upper Egypt.

Gazelles inhabit the desert, and hyenas, foxes, jackals, wild asses, boars, mongooses, and jerboas roam the Nile Delta and the mountains along the Red Sea. The jerboa is a small rodent with long hind legs that enable it to jump distances of up to nine feet.

Birdlife is abundant in Egypt, especially in the delta and valley of the Nile. About

Independent Picture Service

Cliffs composed of sedimentary rock line the banks of the Nile River. Both limestone (compressed shells and skeletons) and sandstone (a hardened mixture of quartz sand) form the rocky terrain.

300 species of birds—including sunbirds, golden orioles, egrets, pelicans, flamingos, herons, storks, and quail—exist in the country. Birds of prey include eagles, falcons, vultures, owls, and hawks. More than 100 species of fish live in the Nile and in the lakes of the delta, providing sport and livelihood for fishermen.

Natural Resources

The cliffs bordering the Nile are composed largely of limestone and sandstone. Harder stones—such as granite, alabaster, and quartzite—are found in the river area. Some deposits of iron ore, phosphate rock, and gold also exist.

During the 1970s, the Israelis—who controlled the Sinai Peninsula after the Six-Day War in 1967—expanded and developed oil fields at Abu Rudeis and in the Gulf of Suez. When the Egyptians regained the region, they took over the oil fields. By 1985 oil accounted for more than half of Egypt's exports.

Cairo

In the early 1990s, as many as 15 million people lived in Egypt's capital city of Cairo. The population has tripled in just 20 years, because people have moved from rural areas to the country's largest urban area. In addition, warfare between Egypt and Israel from 1967 to 1970 led the inhabitants of Ismailia and Suez to flee to Cairo for safety, further increasing the capital's population.

Much of Cairo is influenced by Western-style urban development. Here, international businesses have established their offices around the city's crowded bus terminal.

Courtesy of Ruth Karl

Independent Picture Service

Many older sections of Cairo feature numerous examples of Islamic architecture.

These changes resulted in an intensely overcrowded city, where modernization has not kept pace with the demands of the huge population increase. Some "neighborhoods" in Cairo contain two million people. In poor parts of the city, hundreds of thousands of people live in miserable conditions with no plumbing or electricity.

Although Cairo is a place where ancient and modern ways mingle, these contrasts are often hidden by the confusion and frenzy of the overflowing city. Interspersed with trucks and automobiles driven by middle-class Egyptians are donkey carts and camels. Businesspeople dressed in Western clothing walk alongside Egyptians wearing the long, flowing robes that have been common for centuries.

The hub of Egyptian industry and government, Cairo is also a center of culture and Islamic religious study in the Arab

A woman in traditional Arab dress manages to carry a wide cluster of baskets for sale at a market.

Photo by Beeching/Maryknoll

world. Members of Egypt's middle class live in high-rise housing and shop at modern stores. Beside these twentieth-century structures stand bazaars (street markets), where goods are sold by bargaining and where strict Islamic religious ways persist. Around the Khan al-Khalili bazaar, for example, women often wear veils in observance of traditional Islamic codes of modesty.

Ports

Alexandria—the second largest city in Egypt, with a population of nearly three million people—is situated on the north coast, near the western mouth of the Nile. In ancient times, Alexandria was the greatest commercial city of the Mediterranean world and a focal point of learning. The city still serves as the chief port of Egypt. Alexandria—where Cleopatra once

Courtesy of John Feeney/*Aramco World*

Workers at a candy stall decorated with brightly colored panels await customers on the eve of a traditional holiday in old Cairo.

Courtesy of Steve Feinstein

Situated on a strip of land between the Mediterranean and Lake Mareotis, Alexandria thrives as a port city. Here, boats sail past the mosque of Abu al-Abbas, a thirteenth-century saint. Built in 1943, the mosque rises above the saint's tomb.

reigned as queen—is an attractive, modern city with many academic institutions, parks, libraries, and marble monuments.

The closing of the Suez Canal during the Six-Day War in 1967 nearly halted life in Port Said (population 382,000), which is located at the canal's Mediterranean entrance. The reopening of the canal in 1975, however, fully restored the city's importance, and it continues to flourish, in part because the port does not charge taxes on imports.

Suez (population 265,000) lies at the southern entrance to the Suez Canal, overlooked by the peaks of the Sinai Peninsula. New deposits of oil have been discovered in the area south of Suez, and the city has a large oil refinery. Neighboring Port Taufiq stands on a man-made island and is connected to Suez by a causeway.

Secondary Cities

About 90 miles southwest of Cairo by rail lies Al-Fayyum, the largest natural oasis in Egypt. Waterwheels and water-powered mills abound in Al-Fayyum, where small streams and springs irrigate vineyards and citrus groves.

Asyut (population 291,000) is one of the most important provincial, commercial, and educational hubs in Egypt. For centuries, caravans visited Asyut from the interior of Africa, especially from Sudan, bringing trade items to Egypt. Today Asyut is one of the most modern communities in Egypt, with a high standard of education and its own university.

Farther south along the course of the Nile in Upper Egypt lies Luxor, a resort town with several ancient ruins. Nearby is the site of Thebes, which was once the capital of the Pharaohs. Along the east bank of the Nile is the Temple of Amen (the Egyptian king of the gods) at Karnak, and on the western bank lie the Valley of the Kings, the Valley of the Queens, and the Tombs of the Nobles, where the treasures of Tutankhamen were discovered in 1922.

Aswan stands at the edge of Nubia in southern Egypt and is surrounded by desert. The massive Aswan High Dam adds to the city's importance. Since construction of the dam, Aswan's population has risen from 20,000 to 196,000. Aswan has ancient origins as a frontier town, but its present prosperity dates from the original Aswan Dam, built by the British in 1902. A new fertilizer plant has also boosted the economy of Aswan, and more development is planned.

Courtesy of Steve Feinstein

White water surges from the Aswan High Dam.

Independent Picture Service

Feluccas—fast, narrow vessels with triangular sails—travel the Nile at Aswan.

A huge sculpture of the head of Ramses II rests on the grounds at the Ramesseum, the Pharaoh's burial temple. Ruler of Egypt from 1290 to 1224 B.C., Ramses II ordered extensive construction projects during his reign. Two of his undertakings – the Ramesseum and Abu Simbel – are among the best-known archaeological sites in Egypt.

Photo by Drs. A. A. M. van der Heyden, Naarden, the Netherlands

2) History and Government

Archaeological discoveries of ancient villages and cemeteries in Egypt have revealed that, long before recorded history, people from other parts of Africa and from western Asia cleared and settled the swamps of the Nile Valley. These people cultivated crops, raised livestock, developed art forms, and conducted trade.

About 3100 B.C. an Egyptian king, often referred to as Menes, united the country from north to south as a single nation and made Memphis (near present-day Cairo) the capital. Menes was the founder of the first dynasty (ruling family) of Egypt and was also the first of many Pharaohs

who ruled over Egyptian civilization throughout 30 dynasties. The dynasties have been grouped into Old, Middle, and New kingdoms, with intermediate periods between each kingdom.

During the first two dynasties, sometimes called the Archaic Period, Egyptians began to use hieroglyphics, a form of picture writing. They also built huge tombs, called mastabas, which evolved into the pyramids of later periods. Because the ancient Egyptians believed in life after death, they entombed their dead with provisions for existence in the afterlife. The elaborate tombs contained large rooms packed with furniture, tools, hunting weapons, food, and drink for the deceased to use in the next world.

The Age of the Pyramids

Pyramids appeared during the third dynasty, which began around 2700 B.C. Each king from the next several dynasties built his own massive tomb. Slave laborers designed and constructed twenty large pyramids. The three most impressive structures were built at Giza, near present-day Cairo, for the Pharaohs Khufu, Khafre, and Menkure.

The Pharaohs of this period were absolute rulers who were considered gods on earth, and their civilization was highly developed. The Egyptians were advanced in all the arts and sciences. For example, their remarkable knowledge of geometry is demonstrated by the precision of their architecture.

From 2200 to 2050 B.C. Egypt fell into the turmoil of the First Intermediate Period, when warring families tried to gain the throne, and Pharaohs no longer held

Photo by Drs. A. A. M. van der Heyden, Naarden, the Netherlands

Camel riders provide a measure by which to judge the colossal size of the Great Pyramid at Giza, built by order of Pharaoh Khufu during the twenty-sixth century B.C.

Independent Picture Service

Carvings, such as this one depicting goats feeding at a tree, decorated the tombs of rulers and high officials beginning in the fifth dynasty (2465–2323 B.C.).

supreme authority. The strife forced a decline in commerce and the arts as the unity of Upper and Lower Egypt crumbled. Regional officials, called *nomarchs,* became powerful.

The Middle Kingdom

Mentuhotep II, the last ruler of the eleventh dynasty, reunified Upper and Lower Egypt during his reign from 2060 to 2010 B.C., which signaled the beginning of the Middle Kingdom (2050–1500 B.C.) Despite occasional rebellions, Mentuhotep restored the central power of the throne and established his capital at Thebes (present-day Luxor).

The Pharaohs of the twelfth dynasty showed not only strength but compassion

Independent Picture Service

The Great Sphinx, with the body of a lion and the head of a human, lies in front of the Pyramid of Khafre. Khafre ruled during the fourth dynasty of the Old Kingdom.

Courtesy of Oriental Institute, University of Chicago

A detail of a harvest scene decorates a wall of the tomb of Menna, who kept agricultural records for Pharaoh Thutmose IV during the early fourteenth century B.C.

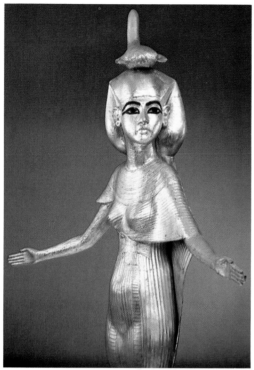

Courtesy of Egyptian Tourist Authority

Found in Tutankhamen's tomb, this gilded wood figure *(above)* depicts Serqet, a scorpion goddess associated with the dead. With her arms outstretched in a protective gesture, Serqet was believed to have special powers over the entrails of the deceased. A bust of Tutankhamen *(below)*, also found in his tomb, is sculpted from pure gold.

Independent Picture Service

as well, promoting an image of themselves as "good shepherds" rather than as remote gods. Amenemhet I and his successors increased Egypt's wealth and power. Military forces conquered Nubia to the south, and Egyptians traded with Palestine and Syria in southwestern Asia. Architecture, literature, and other art forms also flourished during this period.

In the Second Intermediate Period, which lasted from 1800 to 1570 B.C., the dynastic rulers again weakened. Eventually, Egypt was overpowered by the new technology of the Hyksos. Invaders from western Asia, the Hyksos used horses, chariots, armor, and superior weapons to subdue and dominate the Egyptians for over a century.

The New Kingdom

The New Kingdom (1570–1070 B.C.) began when Ahmose I founded the eighteenth dynasty and expelled the Hyksos. Egypt developed a permanent army that used horse-drawn chariots and other military techniques introduced by the Hyksos. With improved weaponry, military forces—led by Thutmose I and by Queen Hatshepsut—entered southwestern Asia. Queen Hatshepsut also increased trade with Africa and saw to the construction of magnificent temples and palaces.

When the queen's successor, Thutmose III, gained control of Egypt around 1480 B.C., his efforts were concentrated on military conquest. Within 20 years he had conquered Palestine and Syria, pushing Egypt's northeastern frontier to the upper waters of the Euphrates River in Asia. One of the greatest triumphs of Egyptian might, the expanded empire survived for a century, making Thebes and Memphis political and cultural hubs of the ancient world.

During the mid-fourteenth century B.C. Amenhotep IV began to worship a sun god called Aten. He changed his name to Akhenaten and moved his court from

Photo by Drs. A. A. M. van der Heyden, Naarden, the Netherlands

Begun by Amenhotep III in the fourteenth century B.C., the Temple of Luxor was not completed until 200 years later, during the reign of Ramses II. The massive yet graceful colonnade is the last section of the temple that was finished by Amenhotep III.

Thebes to Tell al-Amarna. Akhenaten's concentration on religious affairs led to neglect of the empire, which enabled the Hittites of Asia Minor (modern Turkey) to take over Syria. Furthermore, priests of the old religion, who worshiped Amen as king of the gods, led revolts within Egypt. Akhenaten's successor, King Tutankhamen, made worship of Amen the official religion again.

During the late New Kingdom, Egypt again prospered, recovering lost territories and renewing trade. King Seti regained Palestine and Syria, and his son, Ramses II, fought the Hittites. But once again, Egypt was unable to retain its power as invaders came by sea from across the Mediterranean. Nubians from the south and Assyrians and Persians from the east dominated Egypt in succession.

Greek and Roman Rule

In 332 B.C. the Greek conqueror Alexander the Great added Egypt to his holdings. During the same year, he founded the

Photo by Drs. A. A. M. van der Heyden, Naarden, the Netherlands

A painting decorates a wall in King Tutankhamen's tomb, which was discovered in 1922. Relatively small when compared to other tombs in the Valley of the Kings, its entrance was long hidden by the debris of the tomb of Ramses VI.

Independent Picture Service

An ancient coin features the profile of Cleopatra VII, who was the last and most celebrated of the Ptolemaic queens. Her family began its rule of Egypt in the fourth century B.C. with Ptolemy, the able general of Alexander the Great.

seaport of Alexandria in the Nile Delta. Under Greek rule, arts and trade flourished, and Alexandria became a hub of learning, religion, and commerce. Egypt's prosperity eventually attracted the Romans, who conquered the country in 30 B.C., making it a Roman province.

The Romans had actually gained a foothold in Egypt several years earlier, when they assumed control of Alexandria. Cleopatra, who became queen of Egypt the same year, kept her throne by charming the Roman rulers—first Julius Caesar and then Marc Antony, whom she married. After Caesar's assassination, a struggle for power arose between his heirs, Marc Antony and Octavian. Octavian defeated Antony and Cleopatra in the naval battle of Actium in 31 B.C. The couple then returned to Egypt where they both committed suicide the following year.

Roman control continued in Egypt for several centuries. To control the people and to satisfy the powerful priesthood in Egypt, Roman rulers—who were Christians after Constantine the Great legalized Christianity in A.D. 313—protected the ancient Egyptian worship of Amen. Gradually, however, Egypt became an important center for Christianity and developed its own sect, called the Coptic Church, in the fifth century A.D.

Early Arab Rulers

Islam appeared as the world's third major monotheistic (single-god) religion—after Judaism and Christianity—during the early seventh century. Followers of the new religion were called Muslims. Based on the teachings of the prophet Muhammad, Islam spread quickly from Arabia into Syria and Palestine, and then into Egypt. Egypt was very important to the Arabs because it was the major grain-producing region of their main opponent—the Byzantine, or Eastern Roman, Empire. In addition, Alexandria was a valuable base for the Byzantine navy.

Independent Picture Service

This Coptic church stands near a Roman gateway in Cairo. As the written form of the ancient Egyptian language faded, it was carried on in spoken form by Coptic Christians.

The Coptic church of Al-Muallaqa in Alexandria served as the headquarters of Coptic religious leaders in the eleventh century A.D. The interior of the church is intricately decorated with pointed arches, cedar panels, and see-through ivory screens.

Courtesy of Steve Feinstein

In 639 Egypt fell to the Arab commander Amr ibn al-As, who established a new capital at Al-Fustat (now Old Cairo). Many of the Coptic Christians converted to Islam and began to intermarry with Arabs during the early Arab period in Egypt. The conquest of Egypt launched Arab expansion into North Africa and into Spain. Gradually a Muslim administration that used Arabic as its native language replaced the Byzantine-Greek traditions that had prevailed since the Roman period.

The Arabs administered Egypt first from Damascus, Syria, during the Umayyad caliphate (a Muslim dynasty that lasted from 661 to 750) and thereafter from Baghdad, Iraq, the capital of the Abbasid rulers. In 868 the Abbasid caliph, or Islamic leader, appointed Ahmad ibn Tulun from Turkey as the governor of Egypt. Ibn Tulun ruled wisely and effectively. He also established his own ruling family—taking advantage of a weakening Abbasid government—and controlled an independent empire that included Egypt, Palestine, and Syria. After the last Tulunid ruler, the Abbasids were unable to regain their authority.

The Fatimids

During the tenth century, a rival group to the Abbasids arose west of Egypt, in Tunisia. Called the Fatimids, they pursued an aggressive policy toward other Arab possessions. In 969 the Fatimid leader Jawhar al-Siqilli captured Egypt from Abbasid control. Jawhar immediately laid out a new capital next to the older one at

25

Al-Fustat, and he called the new city Al-Qahirah, or Cairo. It became the Fatimid capital in 973 as well as a major cultural and religious center for the Arab world.

The Fatimid period in Egypt was one of extensive construction of mosques (Islamic houses of prayer), palaces, canals, and other public works projects. The Fatimids founded the oldest university in the world, Al-Azhar, which helped to make Cairo a major center of Islamic learning. Although the Fatimids were of the Shiite Muslim sect, they generally allowed Egyptians, who were predominantly Sunni Muslims, to continue Sunni beliefs.

Later Fatimid rulers, however, faced serious problems. They were unable to control regiments of Berber (northwest African) and Sudanese soldiers within the Fatimid army. Famine in 1065 further weakened Fatimid rule.

Crusaders from western Europe set out to establish Christianity in southwestern Asia during the twelfth century. To stem the flow of Christian armed forces, the Fatimid caliph in Egypt appealed to the sultan (ruler) of Syria in 1169 for assistance. The sultan sent an army, and Saladin, a general in the army, became vizier (a high official) of Egypt. In 1171 he overthrew the Fatimids and established the Ayyubid dynasty, restoring Sunni rule to Egypt. Saladin went on to reconquer Palestine from the crusaders. The Ayyubids remained in control of Egypt until 1250, when they were replaced by the Mamluks.

The Mamluks

The Mamluks were rulers of Turkish, Mongolian, and Circassian origins who had been brought to Egypt as slaves by the Ayyubids. The sultan of Egypt had given the Mamluks special military training. They became his bodyguard and rose to high positions in the army and the government. This power enabled them to take over the sultan's domain. The Mamluks formed a military hierarchy that ruled Egypt from 1250 until 1517.

Under Mamluk control, Egypt gained wealth and territory, expanding its boundaries northward to include Syria, mainland Turkey, and the island of Cyprus in the Mediterranean Sea. The Mamluks also made substantial contributions to Egyptian artistic culture, especially in the forms of bronze and brass work, enameled glass, pottery, and intricately decorated manuscripts.

Courtesy of Steve Feinstein

The elaborate structure of Al-Azhar, which was completed in 971, was the first mosque built in the Fatimid city of Cairo. It also houses the oldest university in the world, offering free instruction, lodging, and meals to students from all over the Islamic world.

Courtesy of Steve Feinstein

A Fatimid mausoleum (above-ground tomb) constructed with bricks still stands in Aswan. The Fatimids, a Muslim dynasty, controlled Egypt during the tenth and eleventh centuries.

Independent Picture Service

Amid the structural remains in the northeastern corner of the Temple of Luxor rises the mosque and tomb of Abu Haggag, a respected Islamic holy man of the twelfth and thirteenth centuries. Abu Haggag settled in Luxor around 1193 and lived to be over 90 years old. Many of his descendants still live in the area.

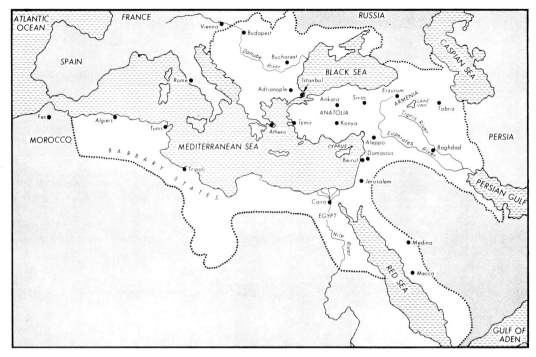

By the seventeenth century, the Ottoman Empire included all of the Middle East, much of the North African coast, and most of Eastern Europe. Because Egypt maintained strong local authority during the Ottoman period, it did not suffer from the severe neglect of most Ottoman holdings. (Map taken from *The Area Handbook for the Republic of Turkey*, 1973.)

Independent Picture Service

Napoleon Bonaparte attempted government reforms while he controlled affairs in Egypt. He also brought with him French scholars, who began a study of ancient Egyptian history.

The Ottoman Empire

In 1517 the Ottoman Turks conquered Egypt and initiated a period of influence that lasted through the middle of the seventeenth century. Although officially claimed as part of the Ottoman Empire until World War I (1914–1918), Egypt retained its own unique identity. Eventually the country governed itself independently of the far-off Turkish empire.

The Ottomans left the country under the control of Turkish officials, called pashas, but the pashas participated little in the Egyptian government. The Ottomans also retained the Mamluks within the local administration. The Mamluks became beys, or regional governors, and held the real power in Egypt.

From the sixteenth to the mid-eighteenth centuries, Egypt prospered because it served as a stopping point along several trade routes between Europe and Asia.

From 1770 to 1800, however, Egypt suffered from plagues and famine, and many Egyptians died.

In 1798 French troops led by Napoleon Bonaparte invaded Egypt to gain control of the land route to the British colony of India. Napoleon captured Alexandria and defeated the Mamluks at the Battle of the Pyramids. Three years later, a combined force of British and Ottoman soldiers drove the French out of Egypt. Although the French occupation was too short to have a lasting effect on Egypt, it renewed European interest in the area and left the country in a state of turmoil.

Muhammad Ali Pasha

By 1805 a powerful figure had emerged in Egypt. Muhammad Ali Pasha—a young Albanian officer who had been sent by the Turkish sultan in 1801 to help oust the French—was appointed governor of Egypt. During the next 40 years, Muhammad Ali began broad reforms to modernize Egypt. He changed the educational system by hiring foreign teachers and established a health and sanitation board to control diseases. He developed manufacturing industries, encouraged the production of cotton, created a modern army, and began to change the way land was distributed.

To gain control of the trade routes into Egypt, Muhammad Ali embarked upon a program of expansion, adding Sudan and parts of Saudi Arabia to his realm around 1820. In 1831 he invaded Syria, defeating the Ottoman armies there, and then headed for Constantinople, the capital of the Ottoman Empire. Russia, Britain, and France intervened to protect the Turkish sultan, but they left Muhammad Ali in control of Syria and the island of Crete. When he rebelled against the sultan again in 1839, the British forced him to give up most of his conquests. The British offered him and his descendants permanent control over Egypt and Sudan instead.

Courtesy of Steve Feinstein

A look through the grillwork of the nineteenth-century Muhammad Ali Pasha Mosque affords a dramatic view of Cairo.

European Intervention

After the death of Muhammad Ali in 1849, Egypt came increasingly under European influence, as careless rulers nearly drove the country into bankruptcy. In 1859 the French Suez Canal Company under Ferdinand-Marie de Lesseps began building the Suez Canal to shorten the water route between Europe and India. The immense task, which took a decade to complete, further drained Egypt's financial resources.

An illustration depicts a line of ships entering the newly opened Suez Canal for the first time.

Egypt agreed to let the Suez Canal Company operate the canal for 99 years. Stock in the canal was owned chiefly by Egypt and France.

In 1875, however, Egypt was forced to sell its share of the company to the British government in order to repay foreign loans. The sale did not prove sufficient to satisfy Egypt's creditors. In 1876 a British-French commission took charge of Egypt's finances, and in 1879 the Ottoman sultan replaced the country's ruler, Ismail Pasha, with his son, Tawfiq Pasha. When the Egyptian army rebelled against foreign control, the British occupied Egypt in 1882. They did not leave until 1956.

Although Egypt technically was still part of the Ottoman Empire when World War I began, Great Britain made the country a protectorate in 1914 after the Ottomans sided with the Germans in the war. Britain's occupation intensified, focusing on the Suez Canal as the keystone to strategic planning in the region.

The war years were very difficult for many Egyptians. Inflation increased, as did resentment toward British control. Egyptian activists formed a nationalist movement called the Wafd (delegation) in 1918. When the British exiled Saad Zaghlul, the Wafd leader, revolt broke out.

Independence

Egypt gained its independence in 1922. Fuad I, the sultan of Egypt, became the new nation's king and worked alongside an elected parliament. Although the country was independent, its foreign policy was still tightly tied to that of Great Britain, and British troops remained in the country. These arrangements robbed Egypt of real independence. Although an Anglo-Egyptian treaty was signed in 1936, British troops remained in the Suez Canal Zone.

Italian and German troops tried to capture the Suez Canal during World War II, (1939–1945) but British forces drove them out. Other nations criticized Britain's rule over independent Egypt, and pressures increased after 1945 for Britain to reduce its influence in the African nation. Fundamentalist (conservative) religious organizations, such as the Muslim Brotherhood, and Communist groups formed as Egyptians became disillusioned with the Wafd party and other internal issues.

Husain Kamil Pasha was given the title of sultan by the British in 1914. At the time of his death in 1917, his brother Fuad became ruler of Egypt.

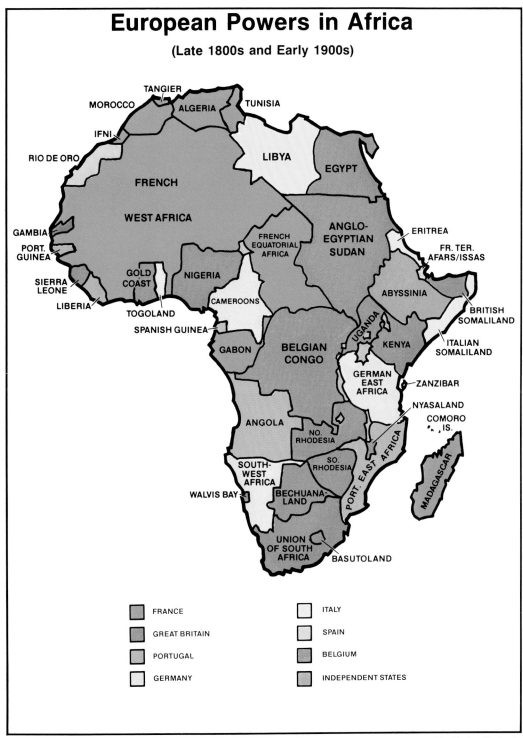

European Powers in Africa

(Late 1800s and Early 1900s)

TANGIER
MOROCCO
ALGERIA
TUNISIA
IFNI
LIBYA
EGYPT
RIO DE ORO
FRENCH
WEST AFRICA
FRENCH EQUATORIAL AFRICA
ANGLO-EGYPTIAN SUDAN
ERITREA
FR. TER. AFARS/ISSAS
GAMBIA
PORT. GUINEA
GOLD COAST
NIGERIA
ABYSSINIA
SIERRA LEONE
LIBERIA
CAMEROONS
TOGOLAND
SPANISH GUINEA
GABON
BELGIAN CONGO
UGANDA
KENYA
BRITISH SOMALILAND
ITALIAN SOMALILAND
GERMAN EAST AFRICA
ZANZIBAR
NYASALAND
COMORO IS.
ANGOLA
NO. RHODESIA
SO. RHODESIA
PORT. EAST AFRICA
MADAGASCAR
SOUTH-WEST AFRICA
WALVIS BAY
BECHUANA-LAND
UNION OF SOUTH AFRICA
BASUTOLAND

FRANCE

GREAT BRITAIN

PORTUGAL

GERMANY

ITALY

SPAIN

BELGIUM

INDEPENDENT STATES

Artwork by Larry Kaushansky

By the late nineteenth century, the Europeans had carved the continent of Africa into areas of influence. British troops occupied Egypt in 1882 and remained in the country until 1956, although it gained nominal independence in 1922. (Map information taken from *The Anchor Atlas of World History*, 1978.)

UPI/Bettmann Newsphotos

Fuad I, son of Ismail Pasha, was born in Cairo in 1868 and was educated in Italy. From 1892 until 1895, Fuad served as a general in the Egyptian army. Nine years before succeeding his brother as head of state, Fuad played an important role in founding Cairo University at Giza. He also served for a time as the institution's president.

In 1945 Egypt and six other nations founded the Arab League and made its headquarters in Cairo. The Arabs looked forward to an era when they could establish Arab unity and could control their own destiny. Conflict within the Middle East, however, was renewed in November 1947. At that time, the United Nations (UN) recommended that Palestine be partitioned (divided) into two states—Jewish and Palestinian Arab.

The Zionist movement—which sought to create a Jewish homeland in Palestine, where ancient Hebrews had lived and developed Jewish culture 2,000 years before —had begun in the late 1800s. Although Arabs had been concerned about Jewish immigration to the region, Great Britain assured them that the new presence did not pose a threat to their territories.

Thus, when the partition plan was announced, the Arab world refused to accept it. Egypt, Syria, Lebanon, and Transjordan (now Jordan) declared war on the new Jewish State of Israel on May 14, 1948. Israel won the war, extending its borders into part of the proposed Palestinian state. Transjordan annexed the rest of the territory that had been set aside for the Palestinian Arabs. Egypt captured the Gaza Strip along the Mediterranean and governed it as a protectorate until 1967. The conflict, however, did not end after the first Arab-Israeli war. Strife directly involving Egypt continued for the next three decades.

The Revolution of 1952

The persistent British presence, the military and political consequences of Israel's creation, and the corruption associated with the regime of King Farouk—who had succeeded Fuad I—eventually caused disturbances within Egypt. Student riots increased, and a military coup took place on July 23, 1952. Major General Muhammad Naguib and Colonel Gamal Abdel Nasser, who would come to dominate the government, led the coup. In 1953 Egypt was declared a republic, and the following year Nasser assumed the presidency. The new regime immediately embarked on an era of change, starting with redistribution of land, removal of foreign troops, and military reform.

In 1954 the British gave in to Nasser's demands and agreed to remove all of their troops by 1956. An agreement in 1955 assured Egypt of large imports of jet warplanes, rifles, and tanks from the Soviet Union. Although this tie with the Communist bloc worried Western countries, Nasser's policies were more concerned with the Arab world, with Islam, and with African affairs.

Former president Gamal Abdel Nasser waves to a crowd. His decision to limit private ownership of land was based on his belief that government control would strengthen Egypt's economy.

Independent Picture Service

The Suez War

In mid-1956 the United States and Britain withdrew offers made in December 1955 to help build a huge new dam across the Nile River near Aswan. Both countries said Egypt was not strong enough economically to make the costly project a profitable venture. In response, Nasser nationalized (changed to ownership by the Egyptian government) the Suez Canal, which had been owned by Britain and France. In so doing, Egypt could use tolls collected from the waterway to finance construction of the Aswan High Dam. The move angered Britain and France, and

they joined Israel, which had complaints of its own, to attack Egypt in 1956.

During this period, relations with Israel worsened, and Egypt continued to block Israeli ships from both the Suez C anal and the Gulf of Aqaba, cutting off Israel's sea communications to the East. Thus, Israel was a natural ally for Britain and France in their conflict with Egypt. When the Suez War—known in Egypt as the Tripartite Aggression—broke out, Israel quickly occupied most of the Sinai Peninsula. After British and French troops invaded the canal zone, the UN stepped in and ended the fighting. It stationed an emergency

Egyptian guns dominated the entrance to the Gulf of Aqaba before the outbreak of the Suez War.

Independent Picture Service

Artwork by Laura Westlund

The colors of Egypt's flag date from the period just after the fall of the monarchy in 1952. Red represents the blood shed during the revolution, white stands for the country's bright future, and black signifies the years before the coup. The falcon is associated with Muhammad, the founder of Islam.

force on the Egyptian side of the Sinai border and at Sharm al-Sheikh, at the tip of the peninsula.

Although Egypt had been defeated in the war, Nasser was considered a hero by Egyptians and by the Arab world in general. Soon thereafter, Nasser secured financing from the Soviet Union for the Aswan High Dam. The deal began a period of close ties between the Egyptians and the Soviets.

Union with Syria

In 1958 Nasser merged Egypt with Syria to form the United Arab Republic. Although the two countries are separated geographically, Nasser believed that a union between Syria and Egypt might be the first step toward a greater level of Arab unity.

Dissatisfaction set in among Syrians, however, and in 1961 a group of Syrian officers rebelled and declared Syria an independent state. This was a great blow to Nasser, who tried to quell the uprising with his troops, but eventually he accepted the loss of Syria. Egypt, nevertheless, retained the name of the United Arab Republic until 1971, when this name was discarded and the name of Egypt was restored.

The Six-Day War

During the spring of 1967, at Nasser's request, the UN withdrew its troops along the Sinai-Negev border. Nasser then advanced his army and again, as in 1956, closed the Gulf of Aqaba to Israeli shipping. Egypt also signed a military alliance with Syria and Jordan.

Faced with threats of war, Israel attacked all three Arab states at once on June 5, 1967, conquering the Sinai Peninsula from Egypt—as well as other territories held by Jordan and Syria—in six days. The Suez Canal, which was shut down during the fighting, remained closed until 1975. Nasser offered to resign his position after the defeat, but Egyptians still had faith in him and insisted that he remain their leader.

Although the war had ended, fighting continued along the Suez Canal, despite the presence of UN troops. In August 1970, Egypt and Israel agreed to a temporary cease-fire, in the hope of beginning peace talks in the near future. Nasser's sudden death from a heart attack in September 1970, however, disrupted the plans.

Anwar el-Sadat

Anwar el-Sadat, who had been appointed vice president in 1969, succeeded Nasser

Independent Picture Service

Former president Anwar el-Sadat initiated *infitah*—an open door policy—through which he sought to relax government controls over the economy and to encourage private investment. These actions contrasted sharply with those of Sadat's predecessor, Gamal Abdel Nasser.

Courtesy of Steve Feinstein

Demonstrators march down a street in Luxor, anticipating an appearance by then-president Anwar el-Sadat.

Palestinian refugees – who left their homes as a result of the 1967 Six-Day War between Arab nations and Israel – rely on UN programs to provide education and play centers for children.

Courtesy of Emile Andria/UNRWA

as president. Sadat released political dissenters who had been imprisoned by Nasser and set out to liberalize the economy and the regime. He decreased censorship of the press, which Nasser had strictly controlled, and ordered all Soviet military advisers out of Egypt during the summer of 1972.

In October 1973 Egypt and Syria attacked Israel to gain back territories lost in 1967. The two countries took Israel by surprise, attacking on Yom Kippur, the holiest day of the Jewish year. The war ended after 18 days of fighting, when the UN imposed a cease-fire. Although the Egyptian forces performed well at the outset, overrunning part of the Sinai Peninsula, the Israelis had regained the initiative when the cease-fire was called. Nevertheless, Egypt's effective challenge to the 1967 boundaries restored the nation's image of strength, and Sadat felt able to negotiate with Israel.

Peace with Israel

By the summer of 1974 Egypt and Israel had agreed to exchange prisoners and to set up buffer zones using UN forces. These agreements permitted the Egyptians to begin work on reopening the Suez Canal, which occurred in 1975. More significantly, however, the peace negotiations resulted in the return of part of the Sinai Peninsula and provided the basis for the Egyptian-Israeli peace treaty of 1979.

In 1977 Sadat announced his historic decision to go to Jerusalem to address the Israeli Knesset (parliament) about a peace settlement. Although Sadat's visit opened the door to the peacemaking process, it caused many frustrations—including the isolation imposed on Egypt by other Arab states who resented Egypt's negotiations with Israel.

In 1978 U.S. president Jimmy Carter invited Israeli prime minister Menachem Begin and President Sadat to Camp David, Maryland. There they constructed a framework for peace between the two countries.

A treaty—which Egypt and Israel signed on March 26, 1979, in Washington, D. C.—ended their state of war. As a result of the treaty, diplomatic relations between the two nations were established, and Israel returned all of the Sinai Peninsula to Egypt.

After 1979 Sadat met with increasing opposition within Egypt. In addition, the rest of the Arab world had branded him a traitor to the Arab cause against Israel. In response, Sadat restricted the Egyptian press and imprisoned those who spoke against his policies. Many of his opponents were Muslim fundamentalists. On October 6, 1981, members of a Muslim fundamentalist group assassinated Sadat while he was reviewing Egyptian troops.

Courtesy of Munir Nasr/UNRWA

In an attempt to offset unsanitary conditions that arise in overcrowded refugee camps, UN relief agencies have established nutrition and health centers.

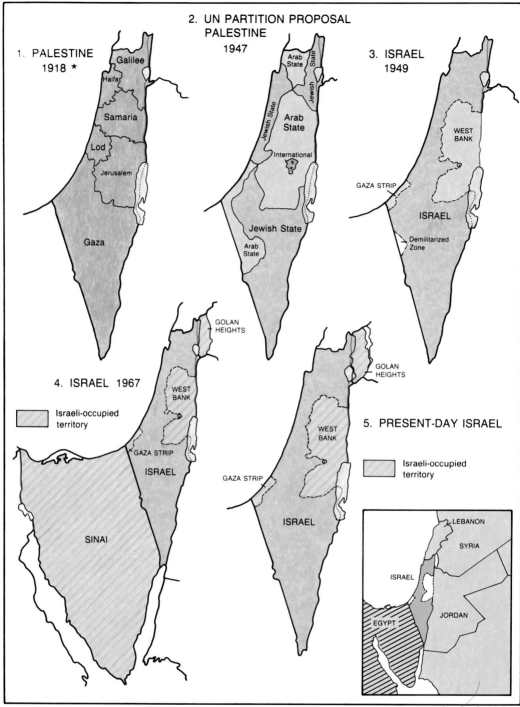

Artwork by Carol F. Barrett

These maps depict the changing boundaries of Palestine and Israel during the twentieth century. Frequently at war with Israel between 1948 and 1979, Egypt has fought and negotiated to maintain control of the Sinai Peninsula. MAP 1 shows the boundaries and internal districts of Palestine under British rule in 1918. MAP 2 outlines the UN's proposal in 1947 to partition Palestine into a Jewish state, an Arab state, and an international zone to be administered by the UN. The cities of Jerusalem and Bethlehem lie within the international zone. MAP 3 shows Israel after the first Arab-Israeli war, with the armistice lines *(dashed)* established in 1949 around the West Bank and the Gaza Strip. Jordan annexed the West Bank after this war, and Egypt claimed the Gaza Strip as a protectorate. MAP 4 illustrates post–Six-Day-War areas occupied by Israel in 1967: the Sinai Peninsula, the Gaza Strip, the West Bank, and the Golan Heights. MAP 5 depicts the present boundaries of Israel and of Israeli-occupied territory. (Israel returned the Sinai Peninsula to Egypt after the peace treaty of 1979.)

*Excluding areas east of the Jordan River.

U.S. president Jimmy Carter looks on as President Sadat *(left)* and Israeli prime minister Menachem Begin *(right)* shake hands at Camp David, Maryland, after their historic peace talks.

Courtesy of Jimmy Carter Library

Courtesy of Embassy of the Arab Republic of Egypt

President of Egypt after Sadat's assassination in 1981, Hosni Mubarak *(above)* has continued Sadat's reform movement. For example, he has greatly increased freedom of the press. A banner in Cairo *(right)* indicates a mood of optimism.

Photo by Andrew E. Beswick

Recent Events

Sadat was succeeded as president by Hosni Mubarak, who had been head of the air force during the 1973 war and vice president since 1975. Mubarak promised to support the peace treaty with Israel and to concentrate more on problems within Egypt. He also strengthened ties with other Arab states. At the Arab summit meeting in November 1987, most Arab leaders agreed to end the isolation imposed on Egypt in 1979. By the late 1980s, Egypt again enjoyed diplomatic relations with nearly all nations in the Arab League.

The early 1990s brought additional international challenges to the Mubarak regime. In August 1990, Iraq invaded Kuwait, an oil-rich nation along the Persian Gulf in the Middle East. The Iraqi army took over the Kuwaiti capital and stationed troops throughout the country. Arab League members were at odds about the appropriate course of action to take. The UN voted to impose economic penalties, called sanctions, on Iraq and left open the possibility of sending an international military force into Kuwait.

Egypt, as well as most other Arab nations, supported the UN sanctions as a means of resolving the Persian Gulf crisis without bloodshed. Eventually, however, Saudi Arabia feared for its own safety. It asked for protection from the United States, which formed a military coalition with several European and Arab nations to reclaim Kuwait. President Mubarak vigorously supported the coalition, sending 30,000 well-trained Egyptian troops to Saudi Arabia.

Egypt's participation had many economic benefits. European, U.S., and Arab leaders erased roughly one-third of Egypt's massive foreign debt. Grants poured in from rich oil-producing Arab states, such as Saudi Arabia, and international banks arranged new loans. In addition, Egypt's own oil industry experienced a boom as warfare cut off oil sources elsewhere in the Persian Gulf.

Independent Picture Service

Egyptian women were granted suffrage (the right to vote) in 1956.

By the time the gulf crisis had ended in mid-1991, Egypt was in a much better economic position. To foster economic progress, Mubarak tried to balance the needs of Egypt's large number of low-income citizens with measures to end subsidies (government payments) for basic consumer goods.

Moreover, Egypt continued to support the idea of a regional peace conference to resolve some of the area's long-standing problems. This stance has again made Mubarak an ally of the United States, which also has been pressing for Middle East talks. Some Egyptian political parties have shown their oppostion to Mubarak's friendly relations with the United States by refusing to participate in national elections. It remains to be seen whether Egypt can maintain its independent position on Arab affairs while continuing to pursue economic progress.

Government

Egypt became a republic after the revolution of 1952. The constitution, last revised in 1971, says that only one person can run for president. At least two-thirds of Egypt's legislature and a majority of the voters must approve the president, who may serve an unlimited number of six-year terms. All Egyptians over the age of 18 are obligated to vote.

The president is commander in chief of the army and may appoint one or more vice presidents and a cabinet. The chief executive may also dismiss these aides and the legislature at any time. The cabinet includes the prime minister and several vice premiers and ministers. This council helps the president to plan and direct national policy.

The Egyptian legislature, which is called the People's Assembly, has 458 members, 448 of whom are elected and 10 of whom are appointed by the president. The constitution reserves 50 percent of the seats for workers and farm laborers. Members of the assembly hold office for five-year terms and are empowered to approve the budget, make investigations, impose taxes, and endorse government programs.

Egypt's independent judicial system is based on elements of Islamic, British, and French laws. In 1956 Egypt became the first Arab country to abolish Islamic and other religious courts. A supreme court is the most powerful of Egypt's four categories of courts. Below the supreme court are the court of cassation (the highest court of appeal), lower courts of appeal, and tribunals.

Each of Egypt's 26 governorates (provinces) is headed by a governor who is appointed by the president. Councils, most of whose members are elected, assist the governors. Cities and villages also have elected councils, which are headed by mayors.

Courtesy of Department of Defense

During the Persian Gulf crisis of 1990–1991, Egyptian military crews practiced maneuvers in the desert of northern Saudi Arabia.

A large percentage of Egypt's population are fellahin, or low-income farm laborers. This fellahin family works the land near Cairo, within sight of the pyramids at Giza.

Courtesy of Steve Feinstein

3) The People

With a population of 54.5 million, Egypt is the most populous country in the Arab world and the second most populous—after Nigeria—on the African continent. Egypt's large population, which is predicted to double in size within 24 years, already puts tremendous pressure on natural resources and food supplies. A huge percentage of Egyptians have low incomes. To support them, the Egyptian government imports much of its food and subsidizes the price of many consumer items.

A large percentage of the gross domestic product (the total value of goods and services produced in the country) is devoted to subsidies.

Three main ethnic groups make up the population of Egypt—Nubians, who moved into southern Egypt from Sudan; descendants of the ancient Egyptians; and Arabs. About 98 percent of the people speak Arabic, Egypt's official language. Most of the population is concentrated in villages and cities along the Nile.

Way of Life

Rural Egyptians make up 55 percent of the total population and are primarily poor farm laborers, called fellahin. A small percentage are Bedouin, who traditionally travel throughout the desert in search of fresh pasture for their sheep and goats. Bedouin usually use camels as their main form of transportation.

The fellahin build homes from mud bricks that have been dried in the sun. They generally live in crowded villages along the Nile River and farm small patches of land. The Egyptian government has sent professionals from Cairo and other large cities to fellahin villages to teach the local people about modern methods of agriculture.

Many of the rural homes in Egypt are made from mud bricks that have been baked in the sun.

Photo by Andrew E. Beswick

Photo by Andrew E. Beswick

Rural villagers pull their boat to the riverbank by means of a rope.

Independent Picture Service

Fellahin thresh piles of grain using oxen *(foreground)*. Less frequently, use of a modern tractor *(upper left)* speeds up the process.

Small groups of wealthy landowners and military officers live in urban areas. Their houses and lifestyles are about the same as those of wealthy people in other parts of Africa or in Europe. Most people who live in Egyptian cities are poor, unskilled laborers. They live in the older sections of town in crowded, tightly packed buildings. Some of these people manage to make enough money to enter Egypt's growing middle class, which is composed mostly of factory owners, merchants, teachers, and technicians.

Health

Health services vary greatly among Egyptians, depending on a family's income and education. Facilities to remove waste and to provide fresh water are often inadequate. In Cairo, for example, many people live without sewers, although the city began construction on a new sewer system in 1985. Many Egyptians suffer from malnutrition because of a poor diet, which often consists of bread made from corn, sorghum (a cereal grain), or wheat; dates; and a small amount of *kishk* (a paste made from sour milk and flour).

Health statistics suggest that conditions in Egypt are average for northern

Independent Picture Service

Bedouin youths whose families have recently settled in permanent towns adjust to their new lifestyle.

A nurse checks the weight of a new-
born baby during a visit to a village
household.

Independent Picture Service

Photo by Beeching/Maryknoll

This woman grinds wheat the traditional way — by crushing the grain between two heavy slabs of stone.

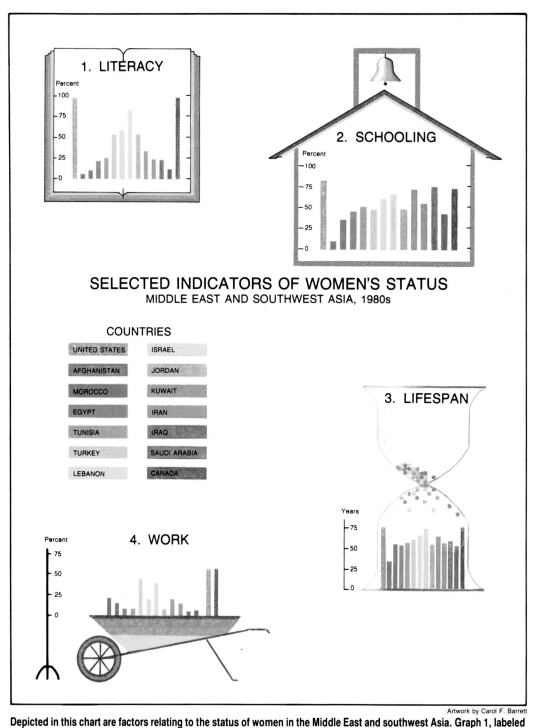

Artwork by Carol F. Barrett

Depicted in this chart are factors relating to the status of women in the Middle East and southwest Asia. Graph 1, labeled Literacy, shows the percentage of adult women who can read and write. Graph 2 illustrates the proportion of school-aged girls who actually attend elementary and secondary schools. Graph 3 depicts the life expectancy of female babies at birth. Graph 4 shows the percentage of women in the income-producing work force. (Data taken from *Women in the World: An International Atlas,* 1986 and from *Women . . . A World Survey,* 1985.)

Africa. The infant mortality rate of 73 deaths for every 1,000 live births and the life expectancy of 57 years of age are about average for the region. The rapid growth in population is also typical. Egypt's 2.9 percent annual rate of population increase is similar to that of other North African countries.

Education

Since Egypt gained independence in the 1920s, the Ministry of Education has been addressing the problem of poor educational facilities. The ministry trains teachers, builds schools, and offers free education from the primary through the university level.

The nation's literacy rate has improved. In the early 1990s, about half the population could read and write. Not enough facilities exist, however, for all children to attend school. Furthermore, some children are unable to attend classes because their parents need them to work in the fields. About 80 percent of all children enter primary school, but only 20 percent continue on to high school.

Courtesy of Kay Chernush/Agency for International Development

Crowded living conditions are a common feature in Egypt's cities.

Some primary-school schedules in Egypt are divided into morning and afternoon sessions. This practice helps to ease crowded facilities and enables more students to attend classes.

Photo by Liba Taylor

Courtesy of Kay Brennan/UNRWA

Young children *(left)* make finger paintings at a play center. Cairo University at Giza *(below)* is an important research institution. Well over 60,000 students are enrolled in the university's various programs of study.

Courtesy of Egyptian Tourist Authority

Most of the postsecondary institutions in Egypt are located in or near Cairo. There are five state universities, which are controlled by the Ministry of Higher Education, and one private university, the American University of Cairo.

Religion

Islam, the faith of more than 80 percent of the Egyptian population, is the official religion of the country. Most Egyptians are Sunni Muslims. Since its founding in the tenth century, Cairo has been one of the great centers for religious study in the Muslim world. The city has more than 1,000 mosques and schools of Islamic learning.

Criers call Muslims to prayer five times a day, and Egyptians are commonly seen praying in mosques, in markets, and in shopping centers. During the month of Ramadan and during other holy days, the recitation of the Koran (Islamic sacred writings) can be heard in city streets over public address systems. The Koran is read on television, and the call to prayer is broadcast on loudspeakers, on radio, and on television.

Islam in its original form combined government and religion. When the modern state system came into existence after World War I, religion became much less important in political affairs. Many contemporary Muslims, however, object to this separation of religious and national functions. These people, generally called fundamentalists, want the sharia, or Islamic law courts, installed as the tribunals of Egypt.

One reason for the growth of fundamentalism is the failure of governments since the 1920s to improve the Egyptian standard of living. Fundamentalists want to develop cooperative organizations to establish more economic equality in Egyptian society. They also believe women should cover themselves as the Koran commands, and they stress the ideals of the past—when Arabs were unified and led the world in scientific achievement. Clashes between fundamentalists and the government have frequently occurred.

Small numbers of various Christian sects also exist in Egypt. Coptic Christians represent the country's largest minority religion. Under Byzantine rule, Egyptians developed their own branch of Christianity and broke away from the Roman Catholic Church during the sixth century. Most other Christians believe that Jesus was one person with two natures—one godly, one human. The Copts believe that Jesus had only a godly nature. Thus, the Copts became known as Monophysites, which literally means "one nature."

Comprising about 15 percent of Egypt's population, the Copts are concentrated in the Coptic section of Cairo, in Luxor, and in Asyut. Tensions occurred between Copts and Muslim fundamentalists in the early 1980s, but President Mubarak has since adopted a policy of toleration toward the Copts.

Courtesy of Minneapolis Public Library and Information Center

Five times a day, a muezzin, or crier, calls Muslims to prayer from the balcony of this minaret (tower) in Cairo.

Photo by Maryknoll Missioners

At a Coptic monastery *(above)* a monk wears the traditional black cloak and hood. A Coptic priest *(left)* begins the traditional ceremony of christening (baptizing and naming a child).

Courtesy of American Lutheran Church

Photo by Liba Taylor

Some families who have made the pilgrimage to Mecca—an Islamic holy city in Saudi Arabia—record their experiences in colorful paintings on the outside walls of their homes.

Literature

Egypt has long oral and written traditions that date back to the ancient Pharaohs. The literary writings of ancient Egypt exhibit a wide diversity of forms and subjects. Some are poems, and others are letters. Still others are collections of moral instructions, which served as school texts that were copied by students to teach them to read and write. Some of the stories use elements of Egyptian mythology and probably originated as part of an oral storytelling tradition. As foreign conquerors took over the region, new styles and themes influenced writing. The literary classics read in Egypt today include Coptic and Arabic contributions as well as ancient works.

European culture has heavily influenced twentieth-century Egypt, stimulating new developments in literature. While traditional writings emphasize detailed descriptions, modern literature strives for balance, unity, and a coherent plot. Contemporary Egyptian authors have adopted European prose forms, such as the short story, novel, and drama. These frameworks are used to discuss problems caused by the introduction of European culture into Egypt. The government has provided financial support to short-story writers, because it recognizes that literature not only spreads culture but also encourages Egyptians to participate in modern life.

Alongside these new forms, however, poetry remains popular, perhaps because it is easily remembered and transmitted by word of mouth. Furthermore, traditional poems were written to entertain ordinary people rather than to appeal to an elite class of educated thinkers.

One of Egypt's leading writers is Taha Hussein. Author of a wide range of books, Hussein supervised the translation into Arabic of the complete works of Shakespeare. Hussein died in 1973 at the age of 84, the day after he received the UN prize for human rights. In 1988 Egyptian novelist Naguib Mahfouz became the first Arabic writer to win the Nobel Prize for literature.

Festivals and Food

Because Egypt is a Muslim country, holidays and festivals follow Islamic traditions. During the month of Ramadan, Muslims fast from dawn to dusk each day. Other festivals relate to historical events in Islam. The Hegira, for example, celebrates the prophet Muhammad's escape from Mecca to Medina in the year 622 and marks the Islamic New Year.

Egyptians consider eating a social event, and meals take time and are prepared with care. A fancy meal may start with an assortment of smoked sardines, stuffed eggs, tiny meat-filled rolls, and beans mixed with pure olive oil. Egyptians eat a great deal of rice and mutton. Yellow saffron rice topped with boiled lamb is a popular dish. Seafood is cooked with tomatoes and pungent herbs. The diet of most Egyptians is based heavily on grains, which they supplement with small amounts of dairy products and fruits, such as dates and figs.

Egyptians prepare highly seasoned foods using a variety of local spices. Menus often include grape leaves stuffed with rice, and olives are placed on the table along with garlic, salt, and pepper. At celebrations, overflowing tables may feature

Photo by Andrew E. Beswick

This girl holds a plate of fresh dates, which are plentiful in Egypt. Dried fruits are also a popular Egyptian food.

a roasted loin of lamb, stuffed spiced chickens, shish kebabs, and continuous supplies of flat, round, freshly baked bread. Salads, fresh fruit, and sweets often complete the meal.

Courtesy of Eliot Elisofon, Eliot Elisofon Archives, National Museum of African Art, Smithsonian Institution

As children look on, a woman prepares a basketful of flat bread over coals in a stone oven.

Independent Picture Service

A farmer on his way to work in the fields plays a simple flute, an instrument that has changed little since ancient times.

Courtesy of Steve Feinstein

Laden with goods, a donkey and fellahin trudge to a market in Luxor.

Courtesy of Steve Feinstein

Schoolchildren line up to visit the treasures of ancient Egypt at the Cairo Museum. The museum's displays include some of the finds from Tutankhamen's tomb.

Courtesy of M. Cherry/FAO

A fellahin transports flour by camel to a food distribution center.

Courtesy of Steve Feinstein

Egyptian women frequently carry water and other goods in jugs balanced on their heads.

Photo by Berceli/Maryknoll

A vendor peddles refreshing fruit drinks on a colorfully decorated cart.

Photo by Drs. A. A. M. van der Heyden, Naarden, the Netherlands

Age-old devices are still used to water Egypt's crops. Here, a camel turns a waterwheel by walking in a circle. Jugs tied to the wheel scoop up water and then pour it into small channels that have been cut into the fields.

4) The Economy

Considered the breadbasket of both the Roman and Byzantine empires, Egypt historically has lived on its agricultural harvests. Even today, the foundation of Egypt's economy rests largely on its six million acres of Nile farmland. About half of the population lives in rural areas and works in the farming sector. Before the revolution of 1952, agriculture accounted for up to 80 percent of the nation's exports. Egypt now, however, must import food to feed its growing population. Agriculture also suffers because the government controls prices. Oil and tourism have replaced agriculture as Egypt's main source of income in the early 1990s.

During the 1970s, former president Sadat began efforts to strengthen the private sector. Laws were passed to attract foreign banks to Egypt and to create favorable incentives for investment. Despite these efforts, the government still runs most big industrial companies and subsidizes the purchase of the majority of basic consumer goods.

In the 1980s, Egypt's economy suffered a decline when oil prices—and the nation's earnings from oil exports—dropped. In the early 1990s, however, the country's oil industry got a boost from the Persian Gulf crisis, which closed off some sources of oil in other parts of the Middle East.

The Mubarak government's decision to help the anti-Iraq coalition during the crisis had several economic benefits. International lenders canceled about one-third of Egypt's large foreign debt, and Arab states sent funds to support the country's war efforts. The lower foreign debt resulted in more international loans, which further eased Egypt's financial woes.

Agriculture

Although only six million acres of Egyptian territory are suitable for farming, a plot of land can produce crops up to three times a year because of the climate. Agriculture has become more regular since the building of the Aswan High Dam, which has eliminated the annual flooding of the Nile Valley.

AGRICULTURAL METHODS

All farmland in Egypt must be irrigated with water from the Nile, since virtually no rain falls. Methods of irrigation have improved little through the centuries. The most common way to water crops is by flood irrigation, in which canals are dug east and west of the Nile, and water is raised into secondary canals by water screws or animal-turned pumps. Occasionally, electric pumps are used.

Photo by Liba Taylor

Another time-honored method of irrigation is the water screw *(above)*. Turning the handle on the screw forces water up curved grooves inside the device and out onto the land. Fellahin collect grain along the banks of the Nile *(right)* as they prepare to send their produce to market. Vital to the Egyptian economy, the Nile River provides the nation with both transportation and the major source of water.

Courtesy of Ruth Karl

Courtesy of Steve Feinstein

An irrigation canal supplies water to a field in Luxor. Smaller canals are dug to carry water from the main source, which allows water to flow to the crops.

Once water has reached the secondary canals, fields are watered by unplugging a hole in a small earthen dike and permitting the field to flood until the water is several inches deep. The dike is then closed. Flood irrigation requires more work than do more modern methods, such as spray or drip irrigation.

Land reform measures instituted after the revolution of 1952 broke up farms, and each farmer was given between two and five acres of land. The small size of the plots plus the use of flood irrigation make it difficult for Egyptian farmers to use mechanized equipment. Tractors and cultivators are rarely seen in Egyptian fields. Traditional farming practices require greater manual labor, which is plentiful in the overcrowded countryside along the Nile.

The absence of modern equipment also necessitates a higher dependency on older forms of transportation, such as the camel or donkey. But although animals do not

Courtesy of Eliot Elisofon, Eliot Elisofon Archives, National Museum of African Art, Smithsonian Institution

Egypt's climate does not provide much grassland for grazing animals. Nevertheless, herds of goats are raised for their meat and milk, as well as for their wool.

Courtesy of Egyptian Tourist Authority

Waterwheels at the Al-Fayyum oasis fill irrigation troughs with water. Oases amid the desert provide fertile areas where Egyptians can raise some crops, such as date palms.

consume oil, they do have to eat. Consequently, part of the agricultural production must go to feed farm animals.

CROPS

Cotton is Egypt's most important crop, and at least 70 percent of it is grown for export. The government, however, stipulates that farmers use no more than one-third of their land for cotton production and that they devote an additional one-third to wheat. The policy seeks to encourage farmers to produce several crops, thereby decreasing Egypt's food imports.

Egypt also produces a wide range of vegetables and cereal crops—sugarcane, potatoes, millet, beans, rice, and onions. With a population that is increasing twice as fast as the rate at which new land is reclaimed for farming, however, the country can no longer meet its food requirements. Sheep, goats, camels, and cattle are raised for meat, as well as for fresh milk and wool. Few farmers raise pigs, since Islamic law forbids the consumption of pork products. Villagers keep chickens for egg production. Water buffalo, horses, donkeys, and camels are kept for working the land.

Courtesy of Agency for International Development

Egypt's population has grown so fast that its agricultural production has not kept pace. This family is well nourished; for many Egyptians, however, malnutrition still poses a problem.

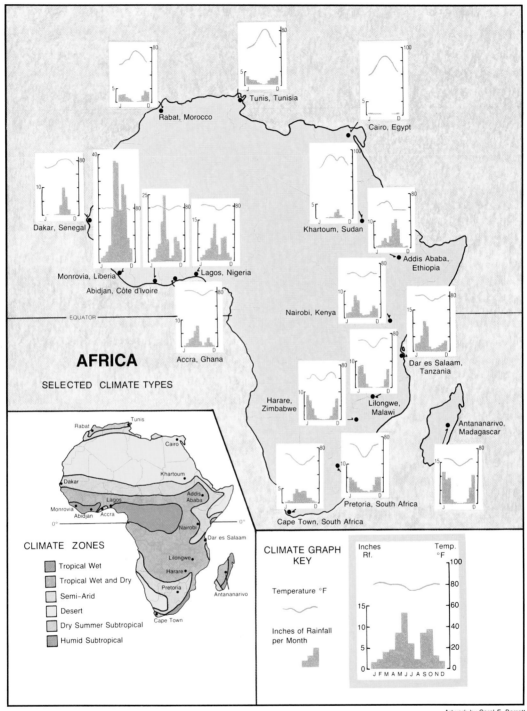

AFRICA

SELECTED CLIMATE TYPES

Tunis, Tunisia

Rabat, Morocco

Cairo, Egypt

Dakar, Senegal

Khartoum, Sudan

Addis Ababa, Ethiopia

Monrovia, Liberia

Abidjan, Côte d'Ivoire

Lagos, Nigeria

Nairobi, Kenya

Dar es Salaam, Tanzania

Accra, Ghana

Harare, Zimbabwe

Lilongwe, Malawi

Antananarivo, Madagascar

Pretoria, South Africa

Cape Town, South Africa

EQUATOR

CLIMATE ZONES

Rabat
Tunis
Cairo
Khartoum
Dakar
Addis Ababa
Lagos
Monrovia
Abidjan Accra
0° 0°
Nairobi
Dar es Salaam
Lilongwe
Harare
Pretoria
Antananarivo
Cape Town

Tropical Wet

Tropical Wet and Dry

Semi-Arid

Desert

Dry Summer Subtropical

Humid Subtropical

CLIMATE GRAPH KEY

Temperature °F

Inches of Rainfall per Month

Inches
Rf.

Temp.
°F

J F M A M J J A S O N D

Artwork by Carol F. Barrett

These climate groups show the monthly change in the average rainfall received and in the average temperature from January to December for the capital cities of 16 African nations. Cairo, Egypt, has a typical low-latitude, desert climate, with average temperatures for the summer months that are well above 90° F. In addition, even the wettest month (December) receives less than one inch of rain, and in some months it does not rain at all. (Data taken from *World-Climates* by Willy Rudloff, Stuttgart, 1981.)

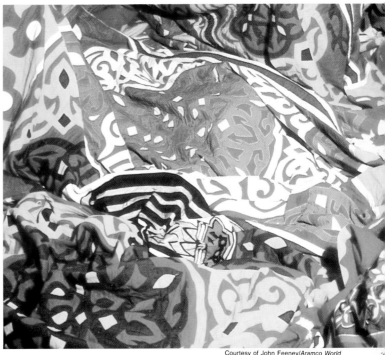

Brilliantly patterned textiles are a common sight at Egyptian markets.

Courtesy of John Feeney/*Aramco World*

Industry

Oil is Egypt's most valuable industrial product. The nation earned $3 billion in 1981 when oil prices were at their highest levels, but that figure dropped significantly when oil prices declined in the mid-1980s. During the Persian Gulf crisis of the early 1990s, Egypt's oil income rose because warfare closed some sources of supply in the Middle East. Furthermore, because the government subsidizes oil prices on the local market, domestic consumption of oil is on the rise. Because the issue of subsidies is sensitive for most Egyptians, the government has tried to avoid making major changes in this practice. Yet economic reforms in 1991 included a cut in the energy subsidy.

After oil, the most important manufacturing industry is textiles. Fabrics produced include cotton and fine woolens. Consumer goods—such as footwear, furniture, stoves, and tourist souvenirs—are manufactured in the cities. Outlying districts produce chemicals, cottonseed oil,

Courtesy of OPIC

At Reynold's International on the outskirts of Cairo, a worker inspects aluminum strips that will be made into pipes. Aluminum processing is a major industry in Egypt.

59

Courtesy of AMOCO

Egypt is increasing its exploration for petroleum, especially in the Western Desert, to help meet Egypt's domestic fuel needs.

and fertilizers. Other major industries include steel, aluminum, military equipment, and sugar refining.

Transportation

Egypt has an extensive railroad network that follows the pattern of settlement along the Nile River. The network includes 2,800 miles of track, running from Alexandria to Aswan. Other lines run east to the Suez Canal and west to the Libyan border.

About 8,000 miles of paved roads and 10,000 miles of gravel roads crisscross Egypt. Most are found in the Nile Valley and are built on a north-south axis. An additional 11,200 miles of dirt roads lead into the desert areas east and west of the Nile. No superhighways exist, and traveling by automobile from Aswan north to Cairo can take a long time because of the number of animals on the road.

Boats, the oldest form of transportation in Egypt, travel on the Nile and its tributaries. Ships ply up and down the 960 miles of the Nile River in Egypt, and canals add another 600 miles of navigable waterways. Dhows and feluccas are traditional sailboats, but the majority of boats are motor-driven. In some places animals walk along the shoreline, pulling flat barges behind them through the water.

Camels carry freight and passengers over desert sands. Among the Bedouin people, camels have traditionally been valued possessions. But even in the great

Traveling by rail through the populous urban centers often means standing on overcrowded passenger cars.

Courtesy of Steve Feinstein

Courtesy of J. Van Acker/FAO

Aswan is not only the location of the Aswan High Dam, which is used for irrigation and power production, but also is an endpoint in road and railway networks.

expanses of the desert, four-wheel-drive vehicles are becoming common and provide quick transport.

Trade

Until the beginning of the twentieth century, Egypt was an agricultural land with a self-sufficient economy. This economy became dependent on foreign trade when cotton became an export crop. Protective tariffs, which were initiated in the 1930s, encouraged the development of Egyptian industry. Nevertheless, exports of manufactured goods remained small and are still limited chiefly to textiles and footwear. Egypt's exports include raw cotton, cotton yarn and fabric, sandals, rice and vegetables, phosphates, manganese ore, mineral oils, and crude oil.

Until the war in 1973, roughly 40 percent of Egypt's exports went to the Soviet Union. After 1973 Egypt's foreign policy changed, which helped turn the flow of trade toward Europe and the United States. Egypt's major trading partners are the United States, Italy, Germany, France, and the Soviet Union.

Tourism

Tourism is one of the largest sources of foreign revenue for the Egyptian economy, bringing in about $1 billion a year. The number of visitors to the country, however, often depends on international events. For example, from 1948 to 1978, when Egypt was frequently at war with Israel, tourism often suffered. Although the industry improved after Egypt signed a peace treaty with Israel in 1979, international terrorism increased during the 1980s, which hurt Egypt's earnings from tourism. The Persian Gulf crisis also caused many vacationers to stay away from Egypt in the early 1990s.

Despite these swings in earnings, Egypt continues to be an important vacation spot. International cruise ships call at the port of Alexandria. In addition, Cairo's airport handles flights from all over the world and is a major transit point to other parts of the Middle East and Africa. For many visitors, however, the most important attractions are found outside Cairo at the ancient pyramid sites of Giza and Saqqara, and at Luxor. Luxor houses the temples of Ramses II and Queen Hatshepsut,

At a brick factory in Luxor, bricks are made by mixing mud with hay and lime. The mixture is then packed into wooden molds and dried by the heat of the sun.

Courtesy of Steve Feinstein

as well as the tombs in the Valley of the Kings dating from about 1500 B.C.

The Future

Despite its great civilizations of the past, Egypt faces substantial challenges in the late twentieth century. The most difficult problems confronting the nation relate to overpopulation. Its 54.5 million people place a tremendous burden on the land, on the country's resources, and on the government to satisfy basic needs. Although efforts are under way to curb the growth rate, the nation's population increases by one million every nine months.

Another area of concern for Egyptian leaders is the economic vitality of the nation. In recognition of its supportive role in the Persian Gulf crisis, Egypt was ex-

Courtesy of Steve Feinstein

An Egyptian guides a felucca full of tourists down the Nile at Aswan.

cused from paying a large part of its foreign debt. International banks have offered more aid in exchange for economic reforms, including a lowering of government subsidies on food and energy.

Egypt's future depends partly on achieving economic progress. The political future of the Mubarak government is tied to the continued support of ordinary Egyptian people, many of whom will be hard hit by the cancellation of subsidies. The nation's leaders face the difficult task of finding the balance between these two goals in the coming decades.

Crowded outdoor market scenes *(right)* typify Egypt's rapid population growth. One of the nation's chief concerns is increasing the size of agricultural yields shipped to local markets *(below)* to meet the needs of the Egyptian people.

Courtesy of Steve Feinstein

Courtesy of Egyptian Tourist Authority

Index